SPORTS CODING CONCEPTS

SPORTY
BUGS AND ERRORS

Allyssa Loya

Lerner Publications ◆ Minneapolis

Lerner Publications Company
An imprint of Lerner Publishing Group, Inc.
241 First Avenue North
Minneapolis, MN 55401 USA

For reading levels and more information, look up this title at www.lernerbooks.com.

Main body text set in Mikado a Regular.
Typeface provided by HVD Fonts.

Library of Congress Cataloging-in-Publication Data

Names: Loya, Allyssa, author.
Title: Sporty bugs and errors / Allyssa Loya.
Description: Minneapolis : Lerner Publications, [2020] | Series: Sports coding concepts | Audience: Age 7–9. | Audience: K to Grade 3. | Includes bibliographical references and index.
Identifiers: LCCN 2019011153 (print) | LCCN 2019018500 (ebook) | ISBN 9781541583634 (eb pdf) | ISBN 9781541576933 (lib. bdg. : alk. paper)
Subjects: LCSH: Software failures—Juvenile literature. | Sports—Juvenile literature.
Classification: LCC QA76.76.F34 (ebook) | LCC QA76.76.F34 L69 2020 (print) | DDC 005—dc23

LC record available at https://lccn.loc.gov/2019011153

Manufactured in the United States of America
1-46712-47706-7/25/2019

Table of Contents

SPORTS, BUGS, AND ERRORS

Have you ever seen a game where a player dropped a ball? Or your favorite player didn't make a shot? Mistakes don't just happen in sports. They happen in coding too.

In sports, coaches tell players what to do. Think of coders as computer coaches. They write lines of code to give a computer instructions. The instructions together make an algorithm. When your coach tells you to shoot a basketball or make a pass, those movements are like algorithms. Just as in sports, algorithms can have mistakes, called bugs. And just as in a game, bugs can mess up the whole algorithm!

In the following activities, you'll fix bugs in players' algorithms to help them win the game! You'll need paper and pencils.

SWISH, SWISH

Swish! You give your body instructions to shoot a basketball. Your shot is like an algorithm. If you miss your shot, your algorithm has bugs.

Get five pieces of scrap paper. Crush each piece into a ball. Then find an empty box or bin. Take five big steps away from the box and turn around. Shoot the paper balls into the box.

On a separate sheet of paper, write down the steps you took to shoot the ball. Those steps are your shot algorithm. How many shots did you make? How many did you miss? Think of each miss as a bug in your shot algorithm. What can you do to fix your shot, or debug it? Try to shoot again. Try to shoot with a partner and debug each other's shots!

SHE SHOOTS, SHE DOESN'T SCORE!

In hockey, the goalie stops the puck from going into the net. She has to move fast with her stick and gloves! Think of her moves as lines of code. If she lets the puck go in, her defense has bugs.

Look at the goalies on page 9. Flying toward each net is a puck the goalie needs to stop. Do you see the arrows below the nets? Each arrow is an instruction, or a line of code, that tells the goalie where to block. Two of these lines of code have bugs. If she follows those instructions, the puck will go into the net. Find the two bugs, and think of how to correct them.

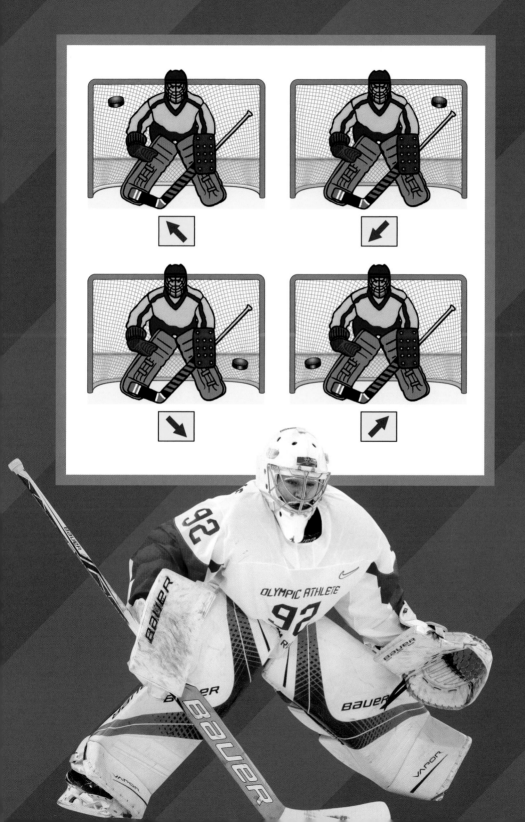

BATTER UP!

Strike three! You're outta here! In baseball, pitchers love hearing those words.

Every batter is good at hitting some pitches and bad at hitting others. Look at the batters on the next page. Imagine you are a pitcher who wants to strike them all out. Each batter has his weakness written in his box. But the instructions for your pitches are all wrong! Debug these lines of code so you can throw three pitches the batter won't be able to hit.

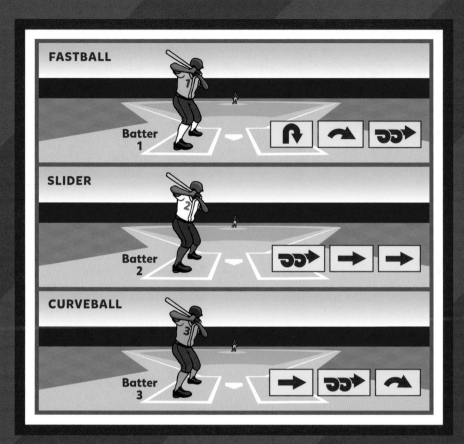

DESIGN FOR THE PROS

Sports jerseys are super cool. How would you like to design one? First, grab a partner. Each of you will secretly pick an animal as your team's mascot. Draw the animal, but don't let your partner see it. Then tell your partner how to draw it, one instruction at a time.

Think of each instruction as a line of code. Your instructions together make an algorithm. Your partner should be able to draw your animal from following your algorithm. If your partner can't guess your mascot, figure out how to debug your code.

FINAL LAP!

Race cars weave in and out around other cars. They need to cross the finish line without crashing. If they crash, that bug ends their whole race!

Grab a partner, and draw a car on four different pieces of paper. Lay the cars down on the floor in front of your partner. Pretend your partner is a car on a track. Without saying anything, use arrows to write an algorithm that will get your partner around all the cars. Hand it to your partner to run. If your partner steps on a car and crashes, the algorithm has bugs. Debug it and try again.

ONE MORE LOOP!

When you and your partner wrote algorithms for the last activity, you might have used the same arrow more than once. In coding, you can use loops to help you repeat the same instruction many times.

In your instructions, did you write ↑↑↑↑ to step forward four times? The same algorithm with a loop looks like this: 4(↑). This means repeat the instruction to step forward four times. Look at your algorithms from the last activity, and turn your lines of code into loops. Then move the cars and write new algorithms, using loops this time. Try adding more cars or changing your track!

GO THE DISTANCE

Long jumpers take many steps to build up speed before they jump. Then they fly through the air as far as they can! The runner who jumps the farthest wins.

The next page shows three long jumpers ready to go. Below each track are two algorithms with loops. The algorithms tell the runner how many steps to run before jumping. Figure out which algorithm, A or B, is the correct one for each track. If the code tells the runner to jump too soon or too late, it has bugs.

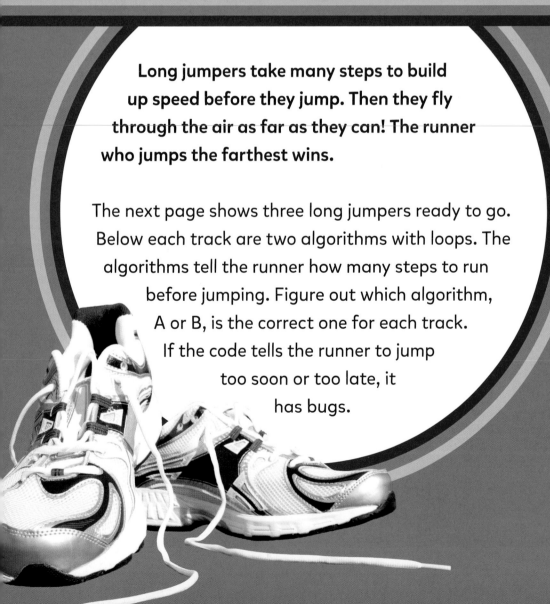

Runner 1

A. 9(➡) ⤴   B. 6(➡) ⤴

Runner 2

A. 7(➡) ⤴   B. 10(➡) ⤴

Runner 3

A. 3(➡) ⤴   B. 5(➡) ⤴

➡ run

⤴ jump

GET IN THE GAME!

Let's play volleyball! When the whistle blows, players need to get to their spots as fast as they can.

Check out the volleyball courts on page 21. Each court has a player ready to run to his spot. Write out an algorithm using loops to get the player to his spot. Run your algorithm. If the player doesn't make it to his spot, you need to debug your code. Look at page 29 to see one possible answer.

TEAMWORK MAKES THE DREAM WORK

It's time to pick your dream team! When you play basketball, it's important to pick the right teammates.

The next page shows a grid of your possible teammates. Each square has a player's name and the player's best trait. Choose the four players you want on your team. Then write four different algorithms with loops to get to your new teammates. If you do not end on the teammate you want, your algorithm has bugs. Debug it and run it again.

good defender	really tall	really fast	good shooter
really fast	good at stealing	good rebounder	good defender
good shooter	really fast	really tall	good shooter
START			

EYES ON THE ROAD!

Cycling is a fast sport. Riders have to make quick decisions so they don't hit anything!

Look at the cyclists on the next page. Then look at the roads in front of them. The riders need an algorithm that will get them around potholes, past other racers, and under hanging branches. Write an algorithm for each racer to get each one safely through the course. You can also use loops. Check your answers on page 29.

↱ Avoid pothole

↳ Avoid branch

↷ Pass other rider

→ Ride straight

GETTING GAME READY

Sports are fun, but you need the right gear to stay safe. Use your coding skills to help a football player get ready for a game.

The football player on the next page is ready to play. He needs to put on five pieces of gear: his helmet, left glove, right glove, left cleat, and right cleat. Write out five different algorithms to get each piece of gear to the right body part. Then check your algorithms for bugs.

Go to page 29 to see some possible answers.

START

Keep Coding!

The next time you're watching or playing a game, think about the mistakes you see. Did a batter strike out? Did a kicker miss a field goal? Mistakes are like bugs in the players' code. Now that you've learned about bugs, you might start seeing them everywhere.

When you see a bug in sports, think about how to correct it. Did a batter change his angle? Did a player adjust his shot? How could the player fix, or debug, the problem? If your parents or siblings are good at sports, ask them how they would fix the mistake. Debug the player's moves together. Then start debugging your own sports algorithms. Fixing your bugs makes you better at both sports and coding!

Answer Key

Pages 8-9: The top right instruction should be ↗.
The bottom right instruction should be ↙.

Pages 10-11:
Pitches to Batter 1 should be
Pitches to Batter 2 should be
Pitches to Batter 3 should be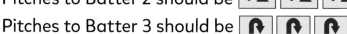

Pages 18-19: Jumper 1: A, Jumper 2: A, Jumper 3: B

Pages 20-21 (possible answer):
Player 1: 4(←), 3(↓); Player 2: 2(←), 4(↑)

Pages 24-25:
Road 1: ⤴ , 2(→), ↗ , → , ⤴
Road 2: 2(→), (⤻), 2(⤴), 2(→), ↗ , →

Pages 26-27 (possible answer):
helmet: 2(←)
right glove: 3(←), 2(↓)
left glove: ←
right cleat: 3(←), 3(↓);
left cleat: ←, 3(↓)

Glossary

algorithm: a group of instructions, made up of lines of code, that tells your computer what to do

bugs: mistakes found in lines of code

code: instructions written for computers to follow

debug: to fix a mistake, or bug, in lines of code

loop: a line of code that tells a computer to repeat an instruction a certain number of times

run: to start an algorithm

Further Information

Code.org: Unspotted Bugs
https://studio.code.org/s/coursea-2018/stage/1/puzzle/1

Funk, Josh. *How to Code a Sandcastle.* New York: Viking, 2018.

Loya, Allyssa. *Sporty Algorithms*. Minneapolis: Lerner Publications, 2020.

Lyons, Heather, and Elizabeth Tweedale. *Learn to Program*. Minneapolis: Lerner Publications, 2017.

Scratch Jr.
https://www.scratchjr.org/

Wonderopolis: "Is a Computer Bug an Insect?"
https://wonderopolis.org/wonder/is-a-computer-bug-an-insect

Index

Photo Acknowledgments

Image credits: Don Mason/Getty Images p. 5 (hurdle); CynthiaAnnF/Getty Images, p. 5 (baseball); FatCamera/Getty Images, pp. 5 (basketball), 23 (athletes); Icon Sportswire/ Getty Images, pp. 5 (hockey), 17; supparsorn/Shutterstock.com, p. 5 (volleyball); Tetra Images/Getty Images, pp. 6, 14 (flag); Westend61/Getty Images, p. 7; walik/Getty Images, p. 8; Sergei Bobylev/Getty Images, p. 9; SERGII IAREMENKO/SCIENCE PHOTO LIBRARY/ Getty Images, p. 10 (helmet); ronniechua/Getty Images, p. 10 (glove); pjohnson1/Getty Images, p. 11; Jeffrey Coolidge/Getty Images, p. 12; Laura Westlund/Independent Picture Service, pp. 9, 11, 13 (illustrations), 15, 17, 19, 21, 23, 25, 27; Tom and Steve/Getty Images, pp. 14 (helmet), 18, 19; Warren Wimmer/Getty Images, p. 15 (cars); creativepictures/Getty Images, p. 20; muuzsy/Shutterstock.com, p. 21; Mr.nutnuchit Phutsawagung/EyeEm/Getty Images, p. 22; Adam Burn/Getty Images, p. 24 (helmet); boschettophotography/Getty Images, p. 24 (wheel); Andrea Kareth/Getty Images, p. 25; Dan Thornberg / EyeEm/Getty Images, p. 26 (both); Tom Merton/Getty Images, p. 27.

Cover: Caroline Schiff/Getty Images (soccer player); Andersen Ross Photography Inc/Getty Images (referee); Lawrence Manning/Getty Images (baseball); Dan Thornberg/EyeEm/Getty Images (football); Chin Leong Teoh/EyeEm/Getty Images (soccer ball); raspirator/Getty Images (background).

About the Author

Allyssa Loya is an elementary school librarian in North Texas and is the author of the Disney Coding Adventures series. Loya has two young boys. She is married to an IT manager, who is a perfect support system for her technological endeavors.